When Life
Seemed Simpler

Boys and Girls
at School

WHEN LIFE SEEMED SIMPLER

DARLING & COMPANY · MMVII

ISBN 978-1-59583-138-5

DARLING & COMPANY
A DIVISION OF LAUGHING ELEPHANT
3645 INTERLAKE AVENUE NORTH
SEATTLE WASHINGTON 98103

WWW.LAUGHINGELEPHANT.COM

INTRODUCTION

Here are gathered pictures, and a few words, from children's school books published between 1930 and 1965. I think that they, concisely and entertainingly, reveal much about the children, the school, the family life, and the attitudes of that era. These readers do differ according to the personality of their makers and the advance of time, but you will see that they present a remarkably consistent point of view.

My thesis is that these schoolbooks constitute a utopian vision. Utopias are imagined societies in which happiness is promoted by a more perfect arrangement of the details of living. They are useful because they give us perfections to aspire toward. The world shown us in these readers is clearly more perfect than the one we inhabit. Everything is clean and orderly. Parents and teachers never lose their tempers, but are, instead, relentlessly helpful and cheerful. Schools are places of adventure, happiness, and joyful learning. Civil servants are anxious to help with any problem, and are especially friendly to children. The young people strive always for the good. They cooperate fully with parents and teachers, and respect authority. They are enthralled with their increasing knowledge of the world and its wonders.

I believe the ideal society shown in these old school books served as a helpful model for the children who learned from them. They would naturally strive for the perfection in the books, and be helped in making good and harmonious lives.

Many times people laugh at the simplicity and idealism shown in these readers. I hope a perusal of *When Life Seemed Simpler* will, at least, change the nature of the laughter from derisive to appreciative. What is there to dislike in this vision of childhood? Who does not want to believe that homes are places of happiness and encouragement? Should schools be shown as less supportive and inspiring? Should people not frequently smile at one another, and should not children be encouraged to see life as a great adventure to be enjoyed with kindly adults and friendly children?

It is often imagined that all the illustrations in readers look the same. As you can see in this volume this is not true. What is the same are the situations, and certainly realism is preferred, but within the constraints of the format many illustrators developed admirable and distinctive styles. This collection is a tribute to their achievements.

– Welleran Poltarnees

FAMILY

Parents are young, attractive and successful. They are focused on the good of their families. Father works at an outside job, where he dresses in a suit and tie. Mother is well dressed at all times and accomplishes the tasks of cooking and cleaning with grace and élan. Everyone is happy to see Father when he comes home. They eat meals together at a large table, while conversing pleasantly. Everyone cheerfully helps with the chores. There is almost always a pet—a dog, a cat, or both. The pet is included in the family harmony. Everyone in the family is imbued with the idea that life is a merry adventure and they are greatly enjoying it together.

Mother

Father

Baby

Ted

Joe

Mary

The family likes this room.
How does Mother take care of this room?

How do Ruth and David help her?
What can the family do in this room?

Washing the car

Tike! Tike!
Here, Tike! Here!

Father

Mother

12

HOME

Most of the families live in modest homes. They have attractive yards, which are well kept. The home is always decorated in a contemporary style. There are never antiques, and there is never clutter. Everything is modest and orderly. The family usually has two children, and always two parents. There are, thus, three bedrooms. There is also a living room, a kitchen, a breakfast room and a dining room. The house is neither in the country, nor in the city, but in a modest and un-crowded suburb. Every family has a car. The dog has a doghouse in the yard. The cat, if there is one, sleeps on a small mat.

17

Mother! Mother!
I am home, Mother!

This is another room in Bill's home. Which room is it? Look for the things that use electric current here. List the things you find. Put them in the same three groups you learned about before.

Work and Fun for All

SCHOOL

The schools in these readers are a wonderland. The children have a deep respect for the authority of their teachers. It is an appreciative and admiring respect. The students are glad to be where they are, and recognize that teachers must be cooperated with if they are to fully impart their wisdom. The activities are extremely varied. Little time is spent sitting at desks. The children are with the teacher cooking or gardening, or building things, painting, or exploring scientific facts through ingenious play, being read to, or just playing. Harmony reigns, and they feel grateful to their teacher for her leadership. (Teachers, in these books, are always women.)

The children play stop and go.

" We stop on red," said Lee.

" We go on green," said Linda.

Do you stop on red?

John and David work on their map.
The children help them.
Miss Mills helps them, too.

Find the hills on the map.
Find the river on the map.

You can make a map, too.
You can make a map of where you live.

COOKIES

This is the way we
make our cookies.
We mix the dough.
hen we roll it out,
en we cut it into
shapes. Then we
in the oven.

29

FRIENDS

Friendship is the norm in this ideal world. Students welcome each newcomer. They all play and work happily alongside one another. There are no isolated children, no bullies, and no shrinking violets. Everyone is glad to be with everyone else. When one travels, the children met along the way are quickly made into friends. When one visits the farm of the uncle and aunt (a frequent occurrence) the cousins one meets are instant friends. After school and on weekends, each child has many happy companions. Growing up is exciting, and every child is glad to have friends to share the experience.

33

A new boy is coming to our school.
He will be in our room.
He will be a new friend.

35

HEALTH, HYGIENE & SAFETY

These very practical issues are explored in many readers. These matters are, naturally, of central importance to all of us, and deserve the space given to them.

The health teaching stresses exercise, nutrition and posture. Friendly vegetables frequently appear to argue their importance.

Hygiene is elaborately explored. The need for baths, hand washing and germ avoidance is imaginatively stressed. Dentists and tooth care are frequently presented.

Safety precautions are urged in great detail. Police officers are shown as guardians of our safety. Traffic and falling are seen as the primary dangers.

WASH before eating

TAKE CARE of **COLDS**

Get plenty of *Sleep*

DRINK WATER

Play Outdoors

DRESS for the **WEATHER**

GET ENOUGH SLEEP

HEALTH EXHIBITS

A GOOD DINNER

Do you know how to stay well?
Do you want to stay well?
Of course you do.
Then you can work and play.
You can go places and do things.

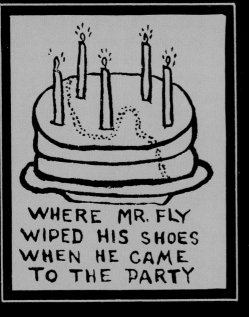

WHERE MR. FLY
WIPED HIS SHOES
WHEN HE CAME
TO THE PARTY

↘ DO YOU KNOW
HOW TO HOLD A
MILK STRAW?

FINGERS
OFF

FINGERS
ON

GUARD
THESE
2
DOORS

GERMS→

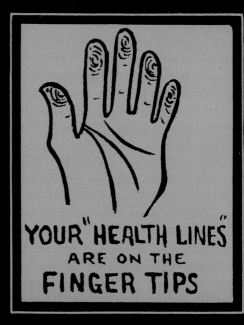

YOUR "HEALTH LINES"
ARE ON THE
FINGER TIPS

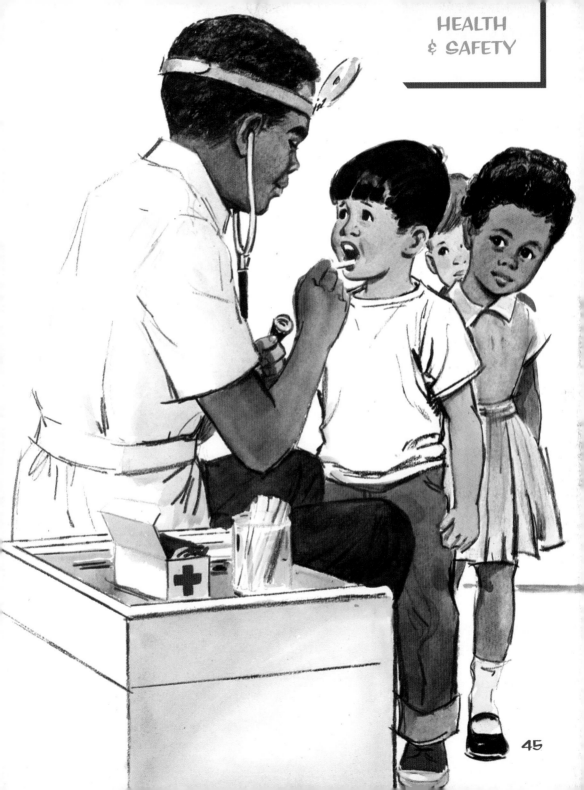

45

46

47

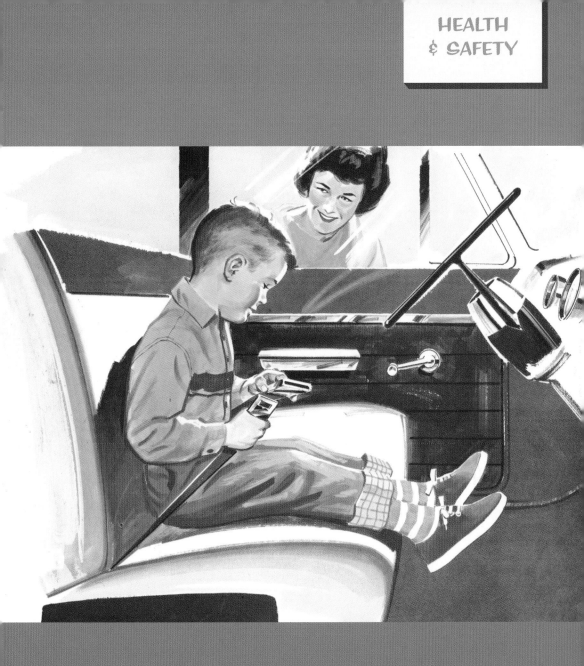

Safety in the Car

THE COMMUNITY

One of the finest aspects of these schoolbooks is their emphasis on community, encouraging gratitude for each person's contributions to our lives. We often forget, in our complex society, how well tasks are distributed and how effectively our needs are met. In readers the children often visit people performing various jobs and are shown how we depend on them. Police, firefighters, mail carriers and farmers are the most frequently singled out, but here and there various other occupations are explored—janitors, grocers, bus drivers, cooks and bakers, miners, truckers, bankers, among many.

The books also encourage the goal of indiviual participation in society, with children being encouraged to do their part through courtesy, gratitude, and helpfulness.

Living in Harmony
with Yourself and Others

51

" The mailman is helping people
most of the time," said Mother.

" He has to walk from house to house
with the mail.

When it is cold, he walks in the cold.

When it rains, he walks in the rain.

He does that so we can have our mail
on time."

" Where are we ? " asked Tiny Tom.

" Where is Mother ? " cried Little Sue.

The kind policeman said, " Come !

I will take you to your mother.

She has been looking and looking

for you."

The children got into the car

with the policeman.

Soon they were on the way home.

55

PLAY

Play is universal in the world evoked by old children's readers. Children play at home, at school, after school, on vacation and every possible occasion. Home play frequently includes the parents. School play is usually instructive, the teachers finding imaginative ways to help children understand the past or scientific principles. After-school play is predictably traditional—baseball, basketball or football. Vacation play, again, includes the parents. Farm visits provide new opportunities, and the ordinary chores are play for city children. Some of the play involves the children imitating adult activities and roles. Anthropologists tell us this is one of the major uses of the play instinct. Pets are often included in games and play.

"Come, Jane," said Billy.
"Come and play."

Jane said, "I want to play.
I can run and jump."

PETS &
OTHER ANIMALS

It is assumed that children and animals have a natural affinity. Every home has a dog or cat, and frequently both. Dogs are the favorites. They pull carts, pretend to be ill, perform in backyard circuses and enjoy auto journeys. Cats mostly just exist. When children visit the farm their animal enthusiasm is unleashed. They play with, and care for, horses and cows and chickens and goats and pigeons and pigs. Rabbits are favorites, at home and on the farm. When animals live in a schoolroom they are used for educational purposes. The children study them, their eating habits, and their daily behavior.

66

69

Here, Kitty.
Come here.
Come, good Kitty.
Good, good Kitty!

How Fast We Grow

The pets grew and grew.
Soon they were big.
They went to live in the woods.
The pets came back every day.
They wanted something to eat.
They wanted to play with Tom
and Judy.

"Look at Flip!" said Susan.
"Flip likes the big red wagon.
He wants to go for a ride in it."
"Funny Flip!" said Tom.

NATURE

As animals are children's favored companions, the outdoors is their natural habitat. Much time is spent in wonderment at the beauty and complexity of creation. Almost every visible phenomena is admired. Geologic formations, insects, fish, animals, trees, grasses, flowers, mushrooms, weather and season changes are frequently explored. The sky with its clouds, and, at night, the pageant of stars, is a subject of both admiration and learning. Vacations are frequently spent in admiring nature. School studies are, naturally, more analytic. At home, potted plants offer pleasure and knowledge, gardening is both useful and productive and many evenings are spent contemplating the sky.

At night you may see the moon in the sky. Sometimes the moon shines very brightly. When you walk outdoors in the moonlight, you can easily see where you are going. You can see houses and trees and bushes. But moonlight is not bright enough to read by. Even with moonlight, we use electric lights in order to see well. Moonlight is never as bright as sunlight.

We can often see stars in the night sky, too. Stars give some light to the earth. But the light that the earth gets from them is not very bright. Sunlight and moonlight are much brighter than starlight.

The children look at snowflakes.
Snowflakes look like stars.

SCIENCE

Most scientific learning takes place in the schoolroom, though field trips offer further opportunities, and parents like to explicate facts and phenomena. Sometimes children are so excited about what they have learned that they continue experimenting on their own. Wonder is the continuing mood, as it is in the observation of nature. The whole range of physical phenomena is examined—soil, rocks, liquids, gasses, plant growth, photosynthesis, and so on. Animals have much to teach us, if correctly observed. Human biology is, naturally, of great interest. The hair, the eyes, the senses, the skin, the nerves, and the blood stream are explicated, but reproduction is scantily treated.

The Five Doorways

Float or Sink

Can you find pieces of rock like these?
Look for some of different colors.
Find some smooth stones
and some that are not smooth.
Look for stones with shiny bits.
There are many different kinds of rocks on earth.
All rocks are made of minerals.
There are many different minerals.
Different minerals make different rocks.

This part of the earth has turned away from the sun. It is night now. You can see the moon and the stars shining overhead. The moon looks bigger and brighter than any of the stars. It seems larger because it is closer to the earth than the stars. Have you ever watched the moon come up? Where does it rise? In what part of the sky does it set?

Away on a Train

VACATION

Vacations, in the world of readers, are flawless paradises in which parents and children spend all their time joyfully together. This is not very different from the modern family vacation, though, of course, the readers do not recognize the stresses and accidents likely to occur. The trips made, at this time, were most frequently made by car, though train and airplane were rare and exciting alternatives. Destinations are always in the continental United States. One of the nicest things about the trips is how many friendly people one met. Train conductors are especially kind. The children who are encountered were glad to play, and promised to become lasting friends. Dogs are included in most auto vacations. The beach is a favorite destination.

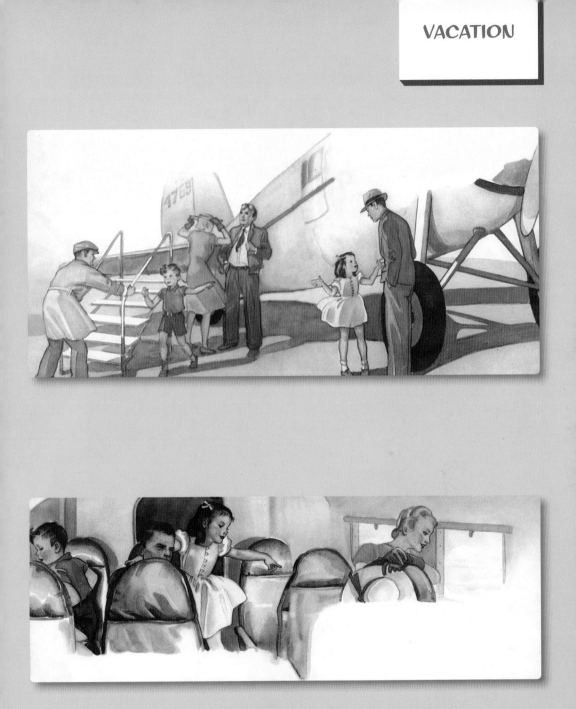

HOLIDAYS

Holidays, then and now, are joyous points of celebration. New Year's Day was a chance to reflect on the opportunities offered by a fresh new year. St. Valentine's Day was perhaps the top school holiday, involving, as it did, hand-crafting cards for all one's friends and parents. Easter was a matter of Easter Eggs and the Easter Bunny. Supplementary eggs were dyed at home or school. Independence Day was celebrated in the schoolroom by historical explorations, and at home with fireworks. Halloween was then, as now, a time for costumes, pumpkins and spooky decorations. Thanksgiving evoked, at school, the feast with the friendly Indians. Christmas, the jewel of holidays, involved extensive preparations for a pageant, gift making, and elaborate decorations for the home.

103

The Party at School

Having Thanksgiving dinner

PATRIOTISM

The children of our reader world are intensely patriotic, like their parents. History is the bedrock, with much attention being paid to Columbus and the pilgrims. The Revolutionary War, The Declaration of Independence and The Constitution are all lovingly examined. The Civil War is for them a very compelling drama, though it occurred many years ago. World War I is, in the earlier readers, a fresh memory for parents, and World War II the same for readers of the later volumes. Armistice Day and Memorial Day are powerful events. An American flag is at the front of most schoolrooms, and every day begins with the Pledge of Allegiance.

111

PICTURE CREDITS

30   Unknown. From *Science for Work and Play,* 1959.

31   Charles and Dorothea Fox and Margo Locke. From *Ginn Elementary English,* 1968.

32   Unknown. From *Your Health,* 1963.

33   Raymon Naylor and Stanley Fleming. From *Building for Health,* 1960.

34-35   Claudine Nankivel and Ed Bradford. From *Stories About Linda and Lee,* 1960.

36   Rhoda Chase. From *Good Friends,* 1938.

37   Gregory Orloff. From *Science Beneath the Skies,* 1951.

38   Florence and Margaret Hoopes. From *Out and About,* 1949.

39   upper   Unknown. From *We Are Neighbors,* 1948.

        lower   Kate Seredy. From *The Health Parade,* 1939.

40   Unknown. From *Health Stories Book Two,* 1934.

41   Unknown. From *Science for Here and Now,* 1965.

42   Unknown. Educational poster, 1961.

43   Unknown. From *Health,* 1966.

44   Walter F. Cobb. From *Chalk Talks on Health and Safety,* 1925.

45   Unknown. Educational poster, 1966.

46   Unknown. Educational poster, 1961.

47   upper   Georgeann Helms. From *Knowing Yourself,* 1954.

        lower   Raymon Naylor and Stanley Fleming. From *Building for Health,* 1960.

48   Guy Brown Wiser. From *We See,* 1947.

49   Unknown. Educational poster, 1965.

50   George Pay and Clifford H. Schule. From *Wide Horizons,* 1954.

51   Unknown. From *Science for Work and Play,* 1959.

52-53   Corinne Malvern and Charlotte Ware. From *These are Our Friends,* 1942.

54   Vera Stone Norman and Pauline Batchelder Adams.
       From Friends for Every Day, 1938.

55   Nellie Farnam and Clarence Biers. From *David's Friends at School,* 1936.

56   Unknown. Educational poster, 1966.

57   Ruth Ives. From *Play With Jimmy,* 1962.

58   Ruth Steed. From *My Little Blue Story Book,* 1948.

PICTURE CREDITS

59   A.F. and Miriam Story Hurford. From *Three of Us,* 1949.

60   Georgeann Helms. From From *Head to Toe,* 1954.

61   Unknown. From *Science for Work and Play,* 1959.

62   A.F. and Miriam Story Hurford. From *Fun With Us,* 1954.

63   Clara Ernst. From *Ride Away,* 1948.

64   A.F. and Miriam Story Hurford. From *Play With Us,* 1958.

65   Unknown. From *Tags and Twinkle,* 1945.

66   Rhoda Chase. From *Jo-Boy,* 1935.

67   Mildred Lyon Hetherington. From *Girls and Boys at School,* 1956.

68   upper   A.F. and Miriam Story Hurford. From *Many Surprises,* 1949.

     lower   A.F. and Miriam Story Hurford. From *Ride With Us,* 1955.

69   Eleanor O. Eadie. From *Bing,* 1950.

70   Miriam Story Hurford. From *Don and Peggy,* 1950.

71-72   Erick Berry and Frederick T. Chapman. From *Along the Way,* 1940.

73   Joyce Hewitt. From *Side by Side,* 1954.

74   Ed. Gordon and Margo Pisillo. From *The Little White House,* 1948.

75   Corinne Pauli Waterall. From *At Play,* 1940.

76   Unknown. From *Science for Here and Now,* 1965.

77   Frederick E. Seyfarth. From *Fall Is Here,* 1948.

78   upper   Florence McAnelly. From *Water Appears and Disappears,* 1953.

     lower   Florence J. and Margaret C. Hoopes.
             From *The New Day In and Day Out,* 1948.

79   Unknown. From *Science Everywhere,* 1954.

80   Florence McAnelly. From *Water Appears and Disappears,* 1953.

81   Florence Liley Young. From *Outdoor Land,* 1931.

82   A. Gladys Peck. From *Round the Year,* 1933.

83   Guy Brown Wiser. From *Sunshine and Rain,* 1944.

84   Unknown. From *Science Far and Near,* 1959.

85   Unknown. From *Science for Work and Play,* 1961.

86   Georgeann Helms. From *Knowing Yourself,* 1954.

87   Unknown. From *Science Everywhere*, 1954.

88   Virginia Bradendick. From *Spring is Here*, 1956.

89   Unknown. From *Science for Work and Play*, 1961.

90   Unknown. From *Science Far and Near*, 1959.

91   Unknown. From *Science for Here and Now*, 1965.

92   Kate Seredy. From *The Health Parade*, 1939.

93   Unknown. From *Science is Exploring*, 1961.

94   Miriam Story Hurford. From *Days of Fun*, 1950.

95   Mildred Lyon Hetherington. From *Girls and Boys at Home*, 1955.

96   upper   Erick Berry and Frederick T. Chapman. From *Along the Way*, 1940.

        lower   Ed. Gordon and Margo Pisillo. From *The Little White House*, 1948.

97   upper   Miriam Story Hurford. From *Days of Fun*, 1950.

        lower   Florence and Margaret Hoopes. From *Open The Door*, 1947.

98-99   Unknown. From *Jim and Judy*, 1939.

100   Virginia Flint. From *Pets and Friends*, 1937.

101   upper   Kate Seredy. From *The Health Parade*, 1939.

        lower   Kay Draper and Constance Heffron. From *Faces and Places*, 1949.

102   A. Gladys Peck. From *Round the Year*, 1933.

103   Ray Quigley and Charlotte Ware. From *Finding New Neighbors*, 1948.

104-105 Jewel Morrison. From *Why We Celebrate Our Holidays*, 1924.

106   Janet Smalley and Jeanne McLavy. From *Stories About Linda and Lee*, 1949.

107   Mildred Lyon Hetherington. From *Girls and Boys at Home*, 1955.

108   Ed. Gordon and Margo Pisillo. From *The Little White House*, 1948.

109   Rhoda Chase. From *Good Friends*, 1938.

110   Claudine Nankivel and Ed Bradford. From *Stories About Linda and Lee*, 1960.

111   Mildred Lyon Hetherington. From *Girls and Boys at School*, 1956.

112   A.F. and Miriam Story Hurford. From *Three of Us*, 1949.

113   Mildred Lyon Hetherington. From *Girls and Boys at School*, 1956.